GRATEFULNESS

A GRATITUDE JOURNAL

Be Happier, Healthier And More Fulfilled In Less Than 10 Minutes A Day

BY AMY J. BLAKE

© Copyright 2016 — Amy J. Blake

ISBN-13: 978-1537408576
ISBN-10: 1537408577

ALL RIGHTS RESERVED.

No part of this publication may be reproduced or transmitted in any form whatsoever, electronic, or mechanical, including photocopying, recording, or by any informational storage or retrieval system without express written, dated and signed permission from the author.

INTRODUCTION

Hey there,

My name is Amy and I will guide YOU through your 100 day journaling gratitude challenge.

It is well established by now and if you picked up this book you probably already know this, journaling as a habit comes along with a multitude of benefits.

Benefits such as:

- Increasing self-confidence
- Sparking creativity
- Discovering yourself
- Evoking mindfulness
- Expanding IQ
- ...
- But more importantly in this case— **Being Grateful!**

And that's the sole purpose of this journal!
To be a guide that will enable you to re-discover yourself and

harness the benefits of gratefulness (*while spending less than 10 minutes a day*).

So I challenge YOU to start your journey of thankfulness TODAY and commit to journal on a daily basis for the next 100 days!

Once finished, I promise you will be amazed by the results. You will be happier, healthier and with a greater sense of fulfillment. You will have experienced the benefits of journaling first hand.

So what are you still waiting for, let's get right to it!

Cheers,
Amy Blake

DAY: 1

DATE: ....

How am I fortunate?

....

....

....

....

....

....

....

....

....

100 DAYS OF GRATEFULNESS

DAY: 2

DATE:

Who do I appreciate? Why?

100 DAYS OF GRATEFULNESS

DAY: 3

DATE:..........................

What material possessions am I thankful for?

....

....

....

....

....

....

....

....

....

100 DAYS OF GRATEFULNESS

DAY: 4

DATE:..........................

What about my surroundings (home/neighborhood/city/etc.) am I thankful for?

....

....

....

....

....

....

....

....

....

100 DAYS OF GRATEFULNESS

DAY: 5

DATE:...........................

What relationships am I thankful for?

....

....

....

....

....

....

....

....

....

100 DAYS OF GRATEFULNESS

DAY: 6

DATE:_____

When did you smile or laugh today? Who or what made you smile?

....

....

....

....

....

....

....

....

....

....

100 DAYS OF GRATEFULNESS

DAY: 7

DATE:........................

What is comfortable about this moment?

....

....

....

....

....

....

....

....

....

100 DAYS OF GRATEFULNESS

DAY: 8

DATE:......................

Who is always there for you and how do you feel about them?

....

....

....

....

....

....

....

....

....

....

100 DAYS OF GRATEFULNESS

DAY: 9

DATE:........................

What's the last song you heard that you enjoyed? How did it make you feel and why?

....

....

....

....

....

....

....

....

....

....

100 DAYS OF GRATEFULNESS

DAY: 10

DATE:...........................

What's the weather like today, and what's one good thing about that?

....

....

....

....

....

....

....

....

....

....

100 DAYS OF GRATEFULNESS

DAY: 11

DATE:............................

How has technology enhanced your life and your connections recently?

....

....

....

....

....

....

....

....

....

100 DAYS OF GRATEFULNESS

DAY: 12

DATE:........................

What's the best thing about your home, and have you taken time to enjoy it recently?

....

....

....

....

....

....

....

....

....

100 DAYS OF GRATEFULNESS

DAY: 13

DATE:...........................

Have you had an opportunity to help someone recently, and how did you feel about that?

....

....

....

....

....

....

....

....

....

100 DAYS OF GRATEFULNESS

DAY: 14

DATE:..........................

How have you made personal or professional progress lately?

....

....

....

....

....

....

....

....

....

....

100 DAYS OF GRATEFULNESS

DAY: 15

DATE: ....

What simple pleasures did (or can) you enjoy today?

....

....

....

....

....

....

....

....

....

....

100 DAYS OF GRATEFULNESS

DAY: 16

DATE:..........................

What modern conveniences (electronics, appliances, etc) do you enjoy that make life easier for you?

....

....

....

....

....

....

....

....

....

....

100 DAYS OF GRATEFULNESS

DAY: 17

DATE:................................

What is the most beautiful thing you saw today?

....

....

....

....

....

....

....

....

....

....

100 DAYS OF GRATEFULNESS

DAY: 18

DATE:........................

What are three things your arms or legs allow you to do that you enjoy?

....

....

....

....

....

....

....

....

....

....

100 DAYS OF GRATEFULNESS

DAY: 19

DATE:...........................

What's the kindest thing someone has done for you lately?

....

....

....

....

....

....

....

....

....

....

100 DAYS OF GRATEFULNESS

DAY: 20

DATE:..........................

How do your friends/family show they care about you?

....

....

....

....

....

....

....

....

....

100 DAYS OF GRATEFULNESS

DAY: 21

DATE:..........................

What is a unique skill/talent you possess that you are thankful for?

....

....

....

....

....

....

....

....

....

....

100 DAYS OF GRATEFULNESS

DAY: 22

DATE:...........................

Who is a person in your life you are blessed to know and why?

....

....

....

....

....

....

....

....

....

....

100 DAYS OF GRATEFULNESS

DAY: 23

DATE:..........................

What am I taking for granted that, if I stop to think about it, am grateful for?

....

....

....

....

....

....

....

....

....

....

100 DAYS OF GRATEFULNESS

DAY: 24

DATE:........................

What opportunities do I have that I am thankful for?

....

....

....

....

....

....

....

....

....

....

100 DAYS OF GRATEFULNESS

DAY: 25

DATE:..........................

What did you today that you enjoyed and feel thankful for?

....

....

....

....

....

....

....

....

....

100 DAYS OF GRATEFULNESS

DAY: 26

DATE:..........................

What do you feel lucky to have that other people do not?
(food, water, warmth, family, friends, health, etc)

....

....

....

....

....

....

....

....

....

100 DAYS OF GRATEFULNESS

DAY: 27

DATE:..............................

What's the last thing you enjoyed with your senses?
(a good meal, a lovely song, a good movie, aromatherapy, etc.)

....

....

....

....

....

....

....

....

....

....

100 DAYS OF GRATEFULNESS

DAY: 28

DATE:...........................

What's your favorite thing (or room) about your home?

....

....

....

....

....

....

....

....

....

100 DAYS OF GRATEFULNESS

DAY: 29

DATE:............................

What happened this month that I am grateful for?

....

....

....

....

....

....

....

....

....

100 DAYS OF GRATEFULNESS

DAY: 30

DATE:...........................

Who are you most grateful for and why?
(parents, children, spouse, husband, friends, pets, etc.)

....

....

....

....

....

....

....

....

....

100 DAYS OF GRATEFULNESS

DAY: 31

DATE:..........................

What have others done that has benefitted my life?

....

....

....

....

....

....

....

....

....

100 DAYS OF GRATEFULNESS

DAY: 32

DATE:..........................

How can I be thankful for the challenges I have experienced? What did I learn for from?

....

....

....

....

....

....

....

....

....

....

100 DAYS OF GRATEFULNESS

DAY: 33

DATE:...........................

How is my life different today than it was a year ago? How can I be thankful for those changes?

....

....

....

....

....

....

....

....

....

....

100 DAYS OF GRATEFULNESS

DAY: 34

DATE:..........................

What insights have I gained that I am grateful for?

....

....

....

....

....

....

....

....

....

100 DAYS OF GRATEFULNESS

DAY: 35

DATE: ....

HOW CAN YOU START CREATING YOUR IDEAL CAREER STARTING TODAY?

....

....

....

....

....

....

....

....

....

....

100 DAYS OF GRATEFULNESS

DAY: 36

DATE:...........................

What happens in your life without you having to think about it? (e.g. the sun rises, your heart beats...)

....

....

....

....

....

....

....

....

....

100 DAYS OF GRATEFULNESS

DAY: 37

DATE:...........................

What did your husband/brother/child do today without you having to ask?

....

....

....

....

....

....

....

....

....

....

100 DAYS OF GRATEFULNESS

DAY: 38

DATE:..............................

What did not exist 10, 30, 50 year ago that is now a regular part of your daily life? (food, education, health system, etc.)

....

....

....

....

....

....

....

....

....

....

100 DAYS OF GRATEFULNESS

DAY: 39

DATE: ....

What were you thanked for today?

....

....

....

....

....

....

....

....

....

....

100 DAYS OF GRATEFULNESS

DAY: 40

DATE:...........................

Tell someone what they truly mean for you? (or write them a thank you card instead)

....

....

....

....

....

....

....

....

....

100 DAYS OF GRATEFULNESS

DAY: 41

DATE:

Ask yourself: Are there really any problems in this moment? (forget past and future and focus on the present)

100 DAYS OF GRATEFULNESS

DAY: 42

DATE:..........................

Who's someone who always really listens when you talk, and how does that affect you?

....

....

....

....

....

....

....

....

....

100 DAYS OF GRATEFULNESS

DAY: 43

DATE: ....

Who has helped you become the person you are today, and what's the top thing you'd thank them for?

....

....

....

....

....

....

....

....

....

100 DAYS OF GRATEFULNESS

DAY: 44

DATE:..........................

What's something that inspired or touched you recently?

....

....

....

....

....

....

....

....

....

....

DAY: 45

DATE:...........................

Has anyone done anything recently that made your job easier, and how?

....

....

....

....

....

....

....

....

....

....

100 DAYS OF GRATEFULNESS

DAY: 46

DATE:...........................

Who have you enjoyed being around recently, and why?

....

....

....

....

....

....

....

....

....

....

DAY: 47

DATE:..............................

How have you used your talents and abilities recently, and what have you enjoyed about doing that?

....

....

....

....

....

....

....

....

....

....

100 DAYS OF GRATEFULNESS

DAY: 48

DATE:........................

What have you learned recently that will help you in the future?

....

....

....

....

....

....

....

....

....

....

DAY: 49

DATE:........................

What's one thing you've experienced recently, that made you feel a sense of wonder and awe?

....

....

....

....

....

....

....

....

....

100 DAYS OF GRATEFULNESS

DAY: 50

DATE:...................

What's something you did well recently, and what qualities or skills enabled you to do this?

....

....

....

....

....

....

....

....

....

....

100 DAYS OF GRATEFULNESS

DAY: 51

DATE:..........................

How many of your basic needs do you not need to worry about meeting today?

....

....

....

....

....

....

....

....

....

....

100 DAYS OF GRATEFULNESS

DAY: 52

DATE:........................

What event or interaction made you feel good about yourself today?

....

....

....

....

....

....

....

....

....

....

100 DAYS OF GRATEFULNESS

DAY: 53

DATE:

What musician or type of music are you most thankful for?

....

....

....

....

....

....

....

....

....

100 DAYS OF GRATEFULNESS

DAY: 54

DATE:........................

What form or art are you most thankful for?
(music, acting, writing, painting, something else?)

....

....

....

....

....

....

....

....

....

....

100 DAYS OF GRATEFULNESS

DAY: 55

DATE:........................

What movie/book/blog /article affected your life for the better recently?

....

....

....

....

....

....

....

....

....

....

100 DAYS OF GRATEFULNESS

DAY: 56

DATE:..........................

What have you seen in nature recently, that made you feel happy, peaceful or free?

....

....

....

....

....

....

....

....

....

....

100 DAYS OF GRATEFULNESS

DAY: 57

DATE:...........................

How has modern medicine improved your life, recently or overall?

....

....

....

....

....

....

....

....

....

....

DAY: 58

DATE:..........................

How does electricity simplify and improve your life? Can you imagine what life would be like without it?

....

....

....

....

....

....

....

....

....

....

100 DAYS OF GRATEFULNESS

DAY: 59

DATE:

What's something you have easy access to that always improves your mood, and how has it improved your life?

100 DAYS OF GRATEFULNESS

DAY: 60

DATE:..................................

What happened this month that you are grateful for?:

....

....

....

....

....

....

....

....

....

100 DAYS OF GRATEFULNESS

DAY: 61

DATE:

What about my environment can I be thankful for?

....

....

....

....

....

....

....

....

....

100 DAYS OF GRATEFULNESS

DAY: 62

DATE:...........................

What are you most grateful for that brings joy to your every day life?

....

....

....

....

....

....

....

....

....

....

100 DAYS OF GRATEFULNESS

DAY: 63

DATE:................................

What book are you most grateful, and why?

....

....

....

....

....

....

....

....

....

100 DAYS OF GRATEFULNESS

DAY: 64

DATE:_____

What color do you feel most thankful for?
Is there a color you can't imagine living without?

....

....

....

....

....

....

....

....

....

100 DAYS OF GRATEFULNESS

DAY: 65

DATE:...........................

Is there a personal flaw or limitation you've come to appreciate?

....

....

....

....

....

....

....

....

....

....

100 DAYS OF GRATEFULNESS

DAY: 66

DATE: ....

What vacation are you most grateful for?

....

....

....

....

....

....

....

....

....

....

100 DAYS OF GRATEFULNESS

DAY: 67

DATE:..........................

What is a life experience (good or bad) that has made you a better person?

....

....

....

....

....

....

....

....

....

100 DAYS OF GRATEFULNESS

DAY: 68

DATE:................................

Who can I thank today, and why?

....

....

....

....

....

....

....

....

....

....

100 DAYS OF GRATEFULNESS

DAY: 69

DATE:..........................

How can I say thank you more?

100 DAYS OF GRATEFULNESS

DAY: 70

DATE:...........................

When did you feel good today? What about that made you feel good?

....

....

....

....

....

....

....

....

....

....

100 DAYS OF GRATEFULNESS

DAY: 71

DATE:................................

Ask yourself: What else could this mean? Focus on an unpleasant recent experience with a new perspective.

....

....

....

....

....

....

....

....

....

....

100 DAYS OF GRATEFULNESS

DAY: 72

DATE: ....

What made you proud today, and why?

....

....

....

....

....

....

....

....

....

....

100 DAYS OF GRATEFULNESS

DAY: 73

DATE: ....

Ask yourself: If I WANTED to be grateful, what COULD I be grateful?

....

....

....

....

....

....

....

....

....

100 DAYS OF GRATEFULNESS

DAY: 74

DATE:..........................

How have your spiritual beliefs or practices fulfilled you recently?

....

....

....

....

....

....

....

....

....

100 DAYS OF GRATEFULNESS

DAY: 75

DATE:...........................

Can you think of any non-physical gifts you've received lately? (someone's time, attention, understanding, support)

....

....

....

....

....

....

....

....

....

....

100 DAYS OF GRATEFULNESS

DAY: 76

DATE:...........................

What about today has been better than yesterday?

....

....

....

....

....

....

....

....

....

....

100 DAYS OF GRATEFULNESS

DAY: 77

DATE:

Have you experienced any blessing in disguise lately?

....

....

....

....

....

....

....

....

....

....

100 DAYS OF GRATEFULNESS

DAY: 78

DATE:................................

If you didn't get what you wanted today, can you identify something in what you got that's worth having?

....

....

....

....

....

....

....

....

....

....

100 DAYS OF GRATEFULNESS

DAY: 79

DATE:..............................

What's improved about your life from this time last year?

....

....

....

....

....

....

....

....

....

100 DAYS OF GRATEFULNESS

DAY: 80

DATE:..............................

What's something you're looking forward to in the future?

....

....

....

....

....

....

....

....

....

....

100 DAYS OF GRATEFULNESS

DAY: 81

DATE: ....

What's something you witnessed recently that reminded you that life is good?

....

....

....

....

....

....

....

....

....

....

100 DAYS OF GRATEFULNESS

DAY: 82

DATE:

What's something you witnessed recently that reminded you that people are good?

....

....

....

....

....

....

....

....

....

100 DAYS OF GRATEFULNESS

DAY: 83

DATE:..........................

What act of kindness has made the greatest difference in your life?

....

....

....

....

....

....

....

....

....

....

100 DAYS OF GRATEFULNESS

DAY: 84

DATE:...........................

Name three days in your life that you feel especially thankful for having lived?

....

....

....

....

....

....

....

....

....

....

100 DAYS OF GRATEFULNESS

DAY: 85

DATE:_____

What is an opportunity, big or small, that I have ahead of me?

....

....

....

....

....

....

....

....

....

100 DAYS OF GRATEFULNESS

DAY: 86

DATE:........................

What did you learn from the most difficult part of yesterday, and how will this benefit you moving forward?

....

....

....

....

....

....

....

....

....

....

100 DAYS OF GRATEFULNESS

DAY: 87

DATE:..............................

What am I able to offer others that I am grateful for?

....

....

....

....

....

....

....

....

....

....

100 DAYS OF GRATEFULNESS

DAY: 88

DATE:...........................

What challenges have I been faced with? What did I learn and how can I be thankful for them?

....

....

....

....

....

....

....

....

....

....

100 DAYS OF GRATEFULNESS

DAY: 89

DATE: ....

What teacher are you most thankful for and why? What did you learn from him or her?

....

....

....

....

....

....

....

....

....

....

100 DAYS OF GRATEFULNESS

DAY: 90

DATE:..........................

What happened this month that I am thankful for?

....

....

....

....

....

....

....

....

....

....

DAY: 91

DATE:...........................

What, from this year, do you feel most grateful for?

....

....

....

....

....

....

....

....

....

100 DAYS OF GRATEFULNESS

DAY: 92

DATE:..........................

How can I say thank you to others, to Mother Earth and tho the universe more often?

....

....

....

....

....

....

....

....

....

....

100 DAYS OF GRATEFULNESS

DAY: 93

DATE:..............................

What place do you feel most grateful for and why?

....

....

....

....

....

....

....

....

....

....

100 DAYS OF GRATEFULNESS

DAY: 94

DATE:........................

What is there about the difficulties I am currently experiencing, that I can be thankful for?

....

....

....

....

....

....

....

....

....

100 DAYS OF GRATEFULNESS

DAY: 95

DATE:..............................

What insights have I gained that I am grateful for?

....

....

....

....

....

....

....

....

....

....

100 DAYS OF GRATEFULNESS

DAY: 96

DATE:..........................

Have you recently imagined a worst-case scenario that didn't actually happen?

....

....

....

....

....

....

....

....

....

....

100 DAYS OF GRATEFULNESS

DAY: 97

DATE:..............................

Who in your life survived something difficult, and how do you feel about the fact they're still here?

....

....

....

....

....

....

....

....

....

100 DAYS OF GRATEFULNESS

DAY: 98

DATE:..........................

What choices have you made in the last five years, that you'd thank yourself for making?

....

....

....

....

....

....

....

....

....

....

100 DAYS OF GRATEFULNESS

DAY: 99

DATE:..................................

Where can I help people more?

....

....

....

....

....

....

....

....

....

....

100 DAYS OF GRATEFULNESS

DAY: 100

DATE:..............................

If this was your last moment on earth, what would you appreciate about?

....

....

....

....

....

....

....

....

100 DAYS OF GRATEFULNESS

CONGRATULATIONS

You made it to the very end! Give yourself a hearty pat on the back, you certainly deserve it!

I know this was only a journal but don't let that diminish its value in any way. YOU devoted more than three months of your life to this and hopefully now you have reached the end, you have already started experiencing the benefits of gratefulness first hand!

Practicing gratefulness daily will enable you to live a happier, healthier and more fulfilling life and I hope this journaling challenge was but the first stepping stone to your journey of thankfulness.

That being said, I wish you the very best moving forward and would love to hear if and how this journal helped you in any way!

To Your Success,
Amy Blake

ALL RIGHTS RESERVED.

No part of this publication may be reproduced or transmitted in any form whatsoever, electronic, or mechanical, including photocopying, recording, or by any informational storage or retrieval system without express written, dated and signed permission from the author.

DISCLAIMER AND/OR LEGAL NOTICES:

Every effort has been made to accurately represent this book and it's potential. Results vary with every individual, and your results may or may not be different from those depicted. No promises, guarantees or warranties, whether stated or implied, have been made that you will produce any specific result from this book. Your efforts are individual and unique, and may vary from those shown. Your success depends on your efforts, background and motivation. The material in this publication is provided for educational and informational purposes. Use of the programs, advice, and information contained in this book is at the sole choice and risk of the reader.

CPSIA information can be obtained
at www.ICGtesting.com
Printed in the USA
BVOW03s1909270917
496110BV00001B/65/P